You've

Again, Gabriel

A play for Christmas

ALISON LEONARD

NATIONAL SOCIETY/CHURCH HOUSE PUBLISHING
Church House, Great Smith Street, London SW1P 3NZ

ISBN 0 7151 4773 0

Published September 1988 for the General Synod Board of Education jointly by the National Society and Church House Publishing.

Performing Rights

Cover design by Cathy Simpson.

Printed in England by Orphans Press Ltd, Hereford Road, Leominster, Herefordshire.

CAST

Gabriel
Everyperson
Mary 1
Mary 2
Mary 3 (who becomes the real Mary)
Stage Manager
Narrator
Melchior
Caspar
Balthazar
Carpenter
Dick, a Shepherd
Shepherd 1
Shepherd 2
Shepherd 3
First Small Angel
Second Small Angel
Joseph
Herod
Priest(s)
Scribe(s)
Innkeeper
Innkeeper's Wife
Mr Smithers
Mrs Postlethwaite

Carpenters, Stage-hands and any number of extras to play more Marys, Villagers, Oxen, Asses, etc.

Note:
Most characters can be played either by girls or boys (though Everyperson should be a girl) and by a cast either all of children or of adults and children together.

If the play is done by a small group, some parts can be doubled: Dick with the Carpenter, Shepherd 1 with the Narrator, Shepherds 2 and 3 with the two small Angels, and the Priest and Scribe with Marys 2 and 3.

About the Author

Alison Leonard was born an Anglican, went to a Methodist school and is now a Quaker. She has had three novels for teenagers published: *The Crest of the Dragon* (Hamish Hamilton), *An Inch of Candle* (Fontana Lions) and *Tinker's Career* (Walker Books) and a fourth, *Gatecrashing the Dream Party,* is to be published by Walker Books in 1989. She has had three plays broadcast and is writing this year's play for the Quaker Youth Theatre. Alison is married with two teenage daughters, and has wide experience of writing workshops with young people in schools.

You've Got It Wrong Again, Gabriel was first performed at the Padgate Studio Theatre, Warrington, Cheshire, on December 10th, 1984, with the following cast:

Gabriel	Iain Foulkes
Everyperson	Nicola Corroboy
First Angel	Daniel Jolley
Second Angel	Christopher Jolley
Mary 1	Julia Brown
Mary 2	Joanne James
Mary 3	Lisa O'Toole
Mary 4	Audrey Armstrong
Mary 5	Andrea Penn
Mary	Rachel Hayward
Stage Manager	Karen Green
Caspar	Graham Hallsworth
Melchior	David Green
Balthazar	Stuart Radley
Carpenter	Wendy Chandler
Narrator	Michelle Bennett
Joseph	Warren Petches
Dick	Stephen Caulfield
First Shepherd	Louise Pritchard
Second Shepherd	Stephen Catterall
Third Shepherd	Jane Yarwood
Herod	Derren Dolphin
Priest	Sonia Cole
Innkeeper	Stephen Catterall
Innkeeper's wife	Jennifer Bradbury

Stage Crew and Herod's Court:
Deborah Tansey, Lyndsey Edwards, Lee Swindells.

Angels: Beverley Lord, Sandra Jays, Angela Brooker, Julie Parfitt, Susan Shaw, Victoria Sargeson, Susan Dean, Carla Richards, Nicola Brown, Catherine Latham.

The play was directed by Steve Titchmarsh.

SO YOU'RE THINKING OF PUTTING ON THE PLAY?

You want to do a Christmas play, but not the standard nativity play that you've done for the last X number of years. You want the play to be about Christmas – about what it really means – but you want to have a bit of fun on the way. All the girls want to play the part of Mary. The boys are fighting behind the scenes or getting embarrassed about the fancy way they have to dress up as kings. The adults are annoyed that they're only asked to do the make-up and the scenery and never get the chance to act.

If you've ever had experiences like these, you'll know what made me write *You've Got It Wrong Again, Gabriel.* The publicity for the first production had the headline, 'Does Christmas make you laugh or cry?' After eight years of conventional nativity plays, I was ready to cry. But what I wanted to do was laugh. And I wanted to ask the real questions – all the questions, right from the little ones, like 'Why does the stable always look so clean, when it's supposed to be full of oxen and asses?' up to the Big One: 'Who really was Jesus's f/Father?'

And Gabriel walked into my mind. He didn't swoop down amid archangelic dazzle; he shuffled on, doubtfully peering round from behind a shy and tatty wing.... 'Er – maybe I could be of assistance here?'

Then in strode Everyperson to meet Gabriel, with a breezy 'Of course you can help! Just tell us what's going on around here!'

So, with constant protests from the Archangel Himself (or is it Herself?) and encouragement from Everyperson, *You've Got It Wrong Again, Gabriel* came to be born and written. Since then it has been performed by older pupils in primary schools and younger children in secondary schools, and by church groups of children from 5 to 15, and by mixed groups of adults and children.

CASTING

We've found that flexibility of casting is one of *Gabriel's* great advantages. Clearly Everyperson should be played by a girl, and it might be a little awkward if Mary were played by a boy or Joseph by a girl. Mr Smithers the Sanitary Inspector and Mrs Postlethwaite the Health Visitor would normally - though not necessarily - be played by adults.

But most of the parts can be played by young or old, male or female. We've had male and female Gabriels, and young and older actors playing Everyperson. One large church group felt that the two major parts should be played on the two different nights by different Gabriels and 'Everypeople', and one of their Gabriels was adult and the other a child. We've had a 'Bethlehem graffiti wall' which declared (correctly) that 'Herod is a GIRL! (and so are two of the kings)'. The Stage Manager can be played by an adult, but everybody knows the kind of grown-up who goes around saying 'Children - how *could* you?' and there's usually a child or teenager who longs to do that on stage.

One cast had a pair of identical twins and used them as the Two Small Angels, which led to hilarious confusion (and a few extra lines) in their scene. Another had a child-Mary and adult-Joseph, but Joseph was well over six foot tall and had to kneel, Victorian-romantic fashion, when playing alongside Mary. If you've got lots of spare players they can be used as an angelic choir, or as extra stage-hands or shepherds.

STANDARD OF ACTING

I've mentioned that extra lines can be added if you want. *Gabriel* lends itself to ad-libbing - very handy if you've forgotten a few lines. Clearly, Mary 1 on page 8 can say the names of any well-known child when she admits that she's been fighting, and any relevant complaints about dress and behaviour can be used when the Stage Manager is doing the final check (page 39). Do take liberties with the play in whatever way is appropriate for your particular circumstances.

It also lends itself to some fairly 'ham' acting. Only the two main actors need to be able to act with any degree of skill. If the others bring out their lines woodenly – well, in a sense that's part of the character of the play. If things go wrong in rehearsal and everyone falls about laughing as a result, that can be incorporated into the performance proper. The 'gold, myrrh and frankenstein' line on page 14 was invented by one of the actors during a school read-through, and we couldn't bear to let it go – so there it stands, in the Official Version.

ANCIENT AND MODERN

In the non-sexist spirit of the play, one group decided to change the words of the carols to cut out the too obviously male-dominant references. But it was no good: the audience ignored the words so carefully composed and printed in their programmes, and carried on singing the words they knew. I'm not surprised: tradition is the essence of the Christmas festival, and in a play which 'sends up' the less meaningful aspects of Christmas it's right that there should be a solid rooting in the familiar ground of Christmas carols.

FINDING THE RIGHT LEVEL

You've Got It Wrong Again, Gabriel starts with a volley of rather unusual curses and ends with a whole-hearted expression of the present-day reality of Christmas. In between, it takes us through panic, pretence, quarrels and fights, teacher-pupil relationships, doctrinal controversy, embarrassment and confusion, Bible text nit-picking, and furious disappointment that Christmas happened *then* and not *now*.

Sometimes, early on in rehearsals, someone is heard to wail – 'But where are we meant to *be*? Are we actually in Bethlehem at the moment, or are we in a school nativity play, or even off on a cloud somewhere?'

The answer to that is: 'Hang on, you'll find the right level after a while.' This isn't a naturalistic play; it isn't a re-enactment in realistic terms. It's an exploration of the different dimensions of the Christmas story: mythical and theological and spiritual and severely practical ('This dump? It stinks!').

From the experience we've had so far, the actors, whatever their age and educational attainment, eventually find whatever level their particular character is operating on at any particular moment. If in doubt, have a go at the Kings' scene (pages 33-35) in front of the whole cast. Each king does a chatty bit with Everyperson, then realises the significance of their gift to the Christ child and stands forward with words which clearly come from the spiritual heart. The rest of the play is like that too. The eternal and the trivial mix together. The character of Gabriel is the character of the whole play: swinging crazily from the utterly trivial to the truly eternal.

YOU NEEDN'T GROW OUT OF CHRISTMAS

As a play, *Gabriel* is meant to be fun, and irreverent. But my intentions were deeply serious. For too long Christmas has been 'for the children' – meaning: something we adults grow out of. What a shame for the adults and what an insult to children! Children are often the more clear-sighted, and adults need to be reminded by their vision.

But we all have an 'Everyperson' in us – a part of us that asks awkward questions, that won't be satisfied with a hasty answer. And we all have a Gabriel, who senses the eternal but who keeps getting hopelessly muddled. In the end, each of these sides of us needs to take a fresh look at the Christmas story. We can easily get caught up in theological controversy or materialistic bustle, and forget that Jesus was born in great poverty to a simple girl in a village in the Middle East two thousand years ago – and that the simple fact of that birth can alter the deep realities of our lives today.

At the end of a performance of *You've Got It Wrong Again, Gabriel,* Mary sings 'What can I give him, poor as I am?' Then the cast and audience sings together the whole of Christina Rossetti's carol. I hope the experience of arguing with Everyperson and muddling with Gabriel and bumbling our way through with the rest of the cast will have given those simple, beautiful words new meaning.

QUESTIONS FOR DISCUSSION

The play isn't meant to be a 'text' to be dissected for analysis. But it does raise a lot of issues which schools or churches might like to use as a springboard for discussion. So we have given some 'Questions for Discussion' at the end. I hope that the adults concerned will not use them as 'educational material' but as a basis for a genuinely questioning group exercise, where each individual makes an exploration – not with the aim of finding the Answer, but simply to go one step further in the spiritual quest which we begin at birth and don't finish till we die. Christmas can be life-changing, and the play will have done its job if it contributes to that process of spiritual change.

ACT I

Music as the audience comes in: 'Messiah', Britten's 'Ceremony of Carols' or other Christmas music.

Music fades as the lights go down.

Piano or orchestra plays the introduction to 'Hark, the Herald Angels Sing'.

Gabriel: *(in the dark)* It's beginning! I'm not ready!

Very dramatically, the last two lines of 'Hark the herald'. A spotlight appears on Gabriel, *who is wearing a skinsuit and gazing at the angel-gear and halo lying a little way away. They have clearly just been flung off in despair.*

Gabriel: Come on now. You're going to get it right this time. Cherubim and seraphim can do it, and you're *Gabriel*.....

Picks up the gear and struggles to get it on. The wings are at the front.

Hell's teeth.....

During these efforts the main lighting grows.

Lucifer's eyebrows.....

Takes it off completely, gets half inside it again. Muffled swearing can just be heard.

Satan's knucklebones.....

Enter Everyperson. *She is wearing jeans and a T-shirt.*

Jaws of Jezebel.....

Everyperson *coughs.* Gabriel *stops. Starts again.* Everyperson *coughs again.* Gabriel *stops again.*

Everyperson: Can I help at all?

Gabriel: *(muffled)* I've a feeling it should go .... this way ....

Everyperson: I'm sorry?

Gabriel: *(getting free)* You're what?

Everyperson: Sorry.

Gabriel: What are you sorry for?

Everyperson: Nothing!

Gabriel: What are we talking about?

Everyperson: I've no idea.

Gabriel: Oh dear, have I got it wrong again? Who are you?

Everyperson: My name's Everyperson.

Gabriel: Every who?

Everyperson: Person. You remember Everyman? He used to be Mr Average of the Stage. Now we've gone non-sexist. Who are you?

Gabriel: I'm Gabriel.

Everyperson: Nice name - Gabriel.

Gabriel: The *Archangel* Gabriel.

Everyperson: Oh, that Gabriel. I've always wondered - are you male or female?

Gabriel: I'm *Gabriel*!

Everyperson: But you've got to be one thing or the other. They never say.

Gabriel: I'm.... well, I'm just.... Does it matter?

Everyperson: Imagine if the shepherds went around telling all the people of Bethlehem – 'The Messiah's arrived, and it's a girl!'

Gabriel: See what you mean. Look, I can't be bothered about that now. I'm supposed to be telling everyone what's going on round here, and they won't believe me unless I'm wearing this gear.

Everyperson: What so special about the gear?

Gabriel: It shows I'm an archangel. It's got wings *(shows them)* – but all the angels have those. Mine have special gold edges.

Two Small Angels *walk on and across the stage, chatting and admiring each other's outfits.*

Everyperson: Can't you delegate? Couldn't that lot do the job for you?

Gabriel: *(seeing the* Angels) Quick! Hide me!

Grabs Everyperson, *hides from the* Small Angels. *In a stage whisper:*

Gabriel: Delegate? The very thought! There is such a thing as respect! Have they gone?

Everyperson: They've gone. What are you making such a fuss about? D'you want me to help you put this stuff on?

Gabriel: Clouds of glory – would you?

Everyperson: Like me to?

Gabriel: Love you to.

Picks up the gear and gives it to her.

Everyperson: Wings at the back – way in here....

Slips it on to Gabriel.

Gabriel: *(baffled)* It's that easy!

Everyperson: Where's your halo?

Gabriel: Over here.

Fetches it, tries it on, gets it wrong.

Everyperson: Like this. There.

Gabriel: There! How do I look?

Everyperson: Splendid. Ready for anything.

Gabriel: Oh.

Everyperson: What's the matter?

Gabriel: The 'anything' I'm supposed to be ready for.

Everyperson: What are you supposed to be doing?

Gabriel: There's this thing, this Event, this vital moment in history, this turning-point in time....

Everyperson: What *is* it?

Gabriel: They're going to call it 'Christmas'. They'll celebrate it all over the world, have holidays for it – parties, presents – make money out of it, even stop fighting wars for it....

Everyperson: And you've got to *do* it?

Gabriel: Not do it. Get it going, be sort of Master of Ceremonies for it. It's terrifying. I'm no good at that sort of thing.

Everyperson: What happens if you make a botch of it?

Gabriel: I can't! I mustn't! Think of it - 'I bring you good tidings of great joy - ' and then forget my lines! Half a minute - 'which shall be to all people, for unto....' It's gone! I can't remember!

Everyperson: You're panicking. Listen. We can practise it, you and I. Tell me what you've got to do, and we'll rehearse it.

Gabriel: But we need lots of others! Shepherds – kings – courtiers –

Everyperson: There'll be people around who can play those. Let's give it a try.

Gabriel: Would you really? Help me? That'd be marvellous. But – isn't it a cop-out? I am all-powerful or something – I am an archangel....

Everyperson: Maybe it'll turn out differently. 'The last shall be first, and the first last.'

Gabriel: Last first? First last?

Everyperson: It's a quotation. Somebody said it.

Gabriel: Who?

Everyperson: Somebody. Now. What have we got to do?

Gabriel: There's usually music going on. Carols. Can there be some, while we're working things out?

Everyperson: Good idea. How about 'O Come, All Ye Faithful'?

Gabriel: OK.

Audience sing 'O Come, All Ye Faithful' while Carpenters *come on with wood, saws and hammers and start making a manger,* Stage-hands *with bundles of straw, cardboard and foil to make a star, etc. General preparations for a nativity play.*

As the music finishes, enter Stage Manager *in ordinary clothes.*

Stage Manager: Who's got the glue? Wayne, I might have known. What d'you mean, Philippa – 'How long is a lamb's tail'? That's not how you spell Bethlehem, Lorraine. *(Etc. ad lib. Exit)*

They go on working quietly while:

Enter, left the two Small Angels, *carrying papers. Enter, right, three or more girls including* Mary 1, Mary 2 *and* Mary 3 *in ordinary clothes.*

First Small Angel: We've got to find someone to play Mary.

Second Small Angel: How many candidates have we got?

First Small Angel: One, two, three *(etc. as necessary)*

Second Small Angel: Line up now. Let's have a look at you.

Mary 1: It's not a beauty contest, you know!

Mary 2: 'Miss Weston-super-Mare is wearing a green lurex bikini'.

The Marys *giggle.*

First Small Angel: Stop that. This is serious.

To second Small Angel:

Which one shall we have?

Second Small Angel: *(pulling out* Mary 2) This one. She's got lovely blonde hair.

Mary 1: Mary wasn't blonde!

First Small Angel: How d'you know?

Mary 1: They were sort of Arab, weren't they? It didn't all happen in England.

Second Small Angel: That's a thought.

Pushes back Mary 2.

First Small Angel: *(pulling out* Mary 1) She's sort of middling, isn't she?

Mary 2: You can't have her! She's always fighting!

Second Small Angel: Do you? Always fight?

Mary 1: Only with Gary Davies – and Sharon Brown, but it's her fault, she starts it –

First Small Angel: That's her out.

Pushes her back.

Second Small Angel: I'm fed up. Let's have this one.

Pulls out Mary *3.*

You're such a good actress, we've decided you're going to be Mary.

Cries of 'That's not fair!' from the others.

Mary 3: I haven't said anything yet!

First Small Angel: Mary doesn't say anything in Nativity plays. You'll do fine.

They take her off left, and the others go off right, grumbling: 'My mum said I was sure to get it,' etc.

Enter the Stage Manager.

Stage Manager: Everyone needed for costume fitting! Off you go, you lot – costume fitting!

Shoos off Carpenters *and* Stage-hands, *and goes off too.*

Enter Gabriel *and* Everyperson.

Everyperson: So. It's what you call the Annunciation.

Gabriel: That's the posh word for me going to see Mary. How am I going to know which is her?

Everyperson: She'll be wearing blue.

Gabriel: How d'you know?

Everyperson: She always wears blue. I don't know why.

Gabriel: So I've found her, in blue. What do I say to her?

Everyperson: Didn't someone tell you what to say?

Gabriel: Well.... *He* did.

Everyperson: Who's 'He'?

Gabriel: 'He'. You know – God. You must have heard of God.

Everyperson: I've heard the word often enough. I mean – God is Love, God Save the Queen, God knows, Lord God made them all. It's very confusing.

Gabriel: Don't you get confused as well, Everyperson, please.

Everyperson: I only wanted an answer to a tiny little question – who's God?

Gabriel: Little question....

Everyperson: What's He like? You've seen Him, you must know.

Gabriel: It's not like that. You don't exactly *see* Him. It's all bright and shining.... like being somewhere glorious, but you can't think where. It's absolutely wonderful – so wonderful that when I come away I can't remember a thing.

Everyperson: Let's try it out, and see if it all comes back. I'm Mary. What can I wear? I've got a little blue hankie.... Here we are.

Takes a crumpled blue hankie out of her pocket, straightens it out and puts it on her head.

Right. Start Annunciating.

Gabriel: 'Hail, thou that art highly favoured.' Does that sound right? D'you think I should be more chatty?

Everyperson: Archangels don't chat. Stick to 'Hail'.

Gabriel: 'Hail, thou that art highly favoured. The Lord is with thee. Blessed art thou among women.'

Everyperson *puts her hands to her face.*

What's the matter?

Everyperson: I'm scared.

Gabriel: Why should you be scared? I'm saying 'God's with you, blessed are you'. You should be thrilled to pieces.

Everyperson: It's *awe* I'm filled with. I'm ever so young and ordinary – I'm not famous, or a princess, not clever even. Wouldn't you be scared?

Gabriel: I suppose so. OK. 'Be not afraid, Mary. Thou shalt conceive in thy womb and bring forth a son, and shalt call his name Jesus. He shall be – '

Everyperson: *(standing up)* Hang on, you're going too fast. What was that you said?

Gabriel: Thou shalt conceive in thy womb and –

Everyperson: That's it. How?

Gabriel: How?

Everyperson: How. We all know where babies come from, and none of that applies. Me and Joseph, we're only engaged, and we're a very clean-living couple.

Gabriel: That's a problem. I can see that.

Everyperson: 'He' must have given you an answer to it. Try and remember. Close your eyes, concentrate, think what He actually said.

Gabriel *closes eyes. Silence.*

It must have been something special, or you wouldn't have been sent. Archangels don't go annunciating –

Gabriel: Sssssh!

Everyperson: – for nothing.

Gabriel: I've got it! (Everyperson *kneels again*) 'The Holy Ghost shall come upon thee, and the power of the Most High shall overshadow thee'.

Everyperson: What does that mean?

Gabriel: What d'you mean, 'mean'?

Everyperson: What's going to *happen,* for heaven's sake?

Gabriel: Wait and see. You're the Handmaid of the Lord. It's called obedience.

Everyperson: That's not good enough. Is this going to be the Holy Ghost's baby, or Joseph's baby, or what? Talking of Joseph, what's he going to say about it?

Gabriel: That's all right. He's got the Joseph bit sorted out – that's what I'm going to do next.

Everyperson: You're not going! You're not getting away with it that easily. Whose baby is it, apart from mine?

Gabriel: *(to heaven)* Oh crumbs, why does it have to be like this? I pictured her all meek, you know. Quiet. Uncomplaining.

Everyperson: I'm not complaining. I just want to know.

Gabriel: Leave it, will you. You get to sing the Magnificat now. Won't that do?

Everyperson: Magnificat? What's that?

Gabriel: It's this glorious song – Mary sang it – how does it go? 'My soul doth magnify the Lord, and my spirit hath rejoiced in God my Saviour – '

Everyperson: 'For He hath regarded the lowliness of his handmaiden'.

Gabriel: That's it. How did you know that?

Everyperson: I've been reading the Bible. But there's lots in it I don't understand – that's why I keep on asking questions. 'He hath put down the mighty from their seats and hath exalted the humble and meek. He hath filled the hungry with good things, and the rich he hath sent empty away'.

Gabriel: Wow.

Everyperson: Quite a heavy programme.

Gabriel: It takes time, you know. Even for God.

Everyperson: Maybe he needs a little help from his friends. Anyway, You've got to go off and see Joseph, haven't you?

Gabriel: And the shepherds – and the kings –

Everyperson: Hadn't you better do the kings straight away? They've got all that journeying to do.

Gabriel: So they have. Right. To the kings!

Everyperson: But no wriggling out of the Joseph bit. He's got to know what's what.

Gabriel: I'll do my best – can't make any promises, though.... *(Exit)*

Everyperson: I wonder what he'll say? Well now. How about some more music? 'We Three Kings' – I think that'd be the right one just now.

She raises her hand to set the music going, then goes out the other side from Gabriel.

The audience sing 'We Three Kings', while the Stage Manager *and* Stage-hands *come on and get on with making the manger and other props.*

Enter Melchior, *fitting himself with a cardboard and foil crown. Enter* Caspar *and* Balthazar. Caspar *starts blacking* Balthazar's *face. As the carol ends:*

Stage Manager: You've got your digital watch on, Balthazar!

Balthazar guiltily removes it.

Melchior: Where are our gifts?

Stage Manager: In the cupboard with the hymn books, fifth shelf up, at the back. *(Exit)*

Caspar: We're not flipping mountaineers, you know!

Balthazar: What are our gifts, anyway?

Melchior: Gold and myrrh and frankenstein.

Caspar: Gold and myrrh and *what*?

Melchior: Frankenstein. That's wrong, isn't it?

Caspar: Idiot! It's *frankincense* - you know, *in*cense! Stuff that smells!

Enter Gabriel, nervously. They stare.

Gabriel: Er – kings? Are you the kings?

Caspar: Um – no. I mean yes. That is – we will be in a minute.

Gabriel: Sorry – mistake – back later.... *(rushes off)*

Balthazar: Funny bloke!

Caspar: I'm glad I'm not an angel. Fancy dressing like that!

Carpenter: Talk about fancy dressing – just look at you!

Melchior: We're meant to be like this!

Caspar: Are you taking the mickey or something?

Carpenter: You do look a load of wallies, you must admit.

Caspar: You're calling us –

Balthazar: A load of....

The three of them advance on the Carpenter.

Carpenter: Just you dare....

The others take sides. Cries of 'Go on – give it to him!' etc. Enter the Stage Manager.

Stage Manager: What's this noise? Children! How could you? In the middle of the season of good-will! Is it too much to expect that at Christmas time you show a little bit of consideration for all the hard work that some of us have put in....

The fighters part and run off and the Stage Manager *follows them, still lecturing.*

Enter Gabriel *and* Everyperson *from different sides.*

Everyperson: Did you get the kings on their way, then?

Gabriel: Yes – er – well....

Everyperson: Don't tell me you got it wrong again, Gabriel.

Gabriel: No – you see, when I found them, I remembered that they don't need me, they only need the star.

Everyperson: So you rigged up a star, did you? In the East, like the Bible says?

Gabriel: That's the trouble. If you put the star *in* the East, then the kings will go *to* the East. But if the kings come *from* the East –

Everyperson: Like the Bible says....

During the next few speeches, Joseph *comes in. He carries a small mirror and fiddles about with his beard which has obviously only just been stuck on.*

Gabriel: – the star has got to be in the *West.* Half a minute, is that right? East – West –

Everyperson: See what I mean about asking questions? Anyway, did they set off?

Gabriel: I think so.

Everyperson: Then did you go and see Joseph? You didn't! You're a lily-livered coward, Gabriel, you really are.

Gabriel: I'm on my way to see him now, honestly.... It's all so embarrassing.

Everyperson: We mustn't let Christmas be embarrassing, must we?

Gabriel: Don't be beastly to me, Everyperson. What am I going to say to him?

Everyperson: You've got to tell him whether it's his baby or the Holy Ghost's baby that Mary's having. If you don't, they'll be quarrelling over their creeds and their doctrines for the next two thousand years.

Gabriel: But how do I *put* it? You can't just go up to a man and say, 'Listen, I've got something ever so pleasant to tell you....'

Everyperson *sees* Joseph. *Lights gradually get stronger.*

'.... Your wife - the woman who's going to be your wife - she's, well, she's going to....' You're not listening, Everyperson! It's suddenly got lighter. Why's that?

Everyperson: It's so that you can see what you're doing. I've got to go now, Gabriel.

Gabriel: Go? And leave me?

Everyperson: When I've gone, turn round, and do what you've got to do.

Gabriel: Do?

Everyperson: Bye! *(Exit)*

Gabriel *turns.* Joseph *and* Gabriel *see each other.*

Gabriel: Oh!

Joseph: Hey!

Gabriel: Um – who are you?

Joseph: I'm only Joseph, but *(kneeling)* I know who you are! How marvellous – I'm so honoured – I never in my life thought I'd be visited by the real –

Gabriel: You're *Joseph*?

Joseph: Yes – I'm a carpenter in Nazareth, but now I've been told I've got to trek all the way to Bethlehem – Bethlehem, of all places! – just to pay my taxes, and I'm ever so old and –

Gabriel: The one who's engaged to Mary?

Joseph: I was amazed she'd have me, with me being so old and that. And now here's an archangel come to see me! I feel overwhelmed.... *(he almost prostrates himself)*

Gabriel: Joseph, I've got something to tell you –

Joseph: *(coming up again)* And you're Gabriel, aren't you? Not an ordinary angel – not even the archangel Michael – but the very top one of all – Gabriel! Who'd've believed that humble old me would –

Gabriel: Look, you're not going to be humble, you're going to be famous in a way –

Joseph: Famous? Me?

Gabriel: Well, not you, really – Mary....

Joseph: Mary is? To tell you the truth, Gabriel, I'm not surprised. She's a lovely girl. Have you met her? She's –

Gabriel: Will you shut up for a second and listen to me?

Joseph: Oh! Yes – I'm sorry, how dreadful of me, to chatter on as if you were just....

Gabriel: That's better. Now listen. Mary's going to have a baby –

Joseph: *(jumping up)* A baby! That's terrific! I never dared to hope – with me being so old – Really? You mean it?

Gabriel: Yes. Now, the thing is that –

Joseph: No wonder they sent an archangel! That's thrilling news. How can I ever thank you, Gabriel? Our baby's going to be quite something, I can tell you. Exceptional. I know you'll think I'm just being the proud father, but I know he'll be the greatest, our boy. It will be a boy, won't it? I must run and tell Mary.... *(runs off)*

Gabriel: I've already been to tell.... What happened? Where did I go wrong? Everyperson! Where are you?

Everyperson *comes back.*

Everyperson: What's the matter? Where's Joseph? How did it go?

Gabriel: I don't know! He was ever so sweet, but he just chatted on. I couldn't get a word in edgeways!

Everyperson: You mean you didn't tell him?

Gabriel: I got as far as 'Mary's going to have a baby'.

Everyperson: And he left it at that?

Gabriel: Jumped with joy, and ran off.

Everyperson: He didn't say 'We're a clean-living couple'? Didn't want to know *how?*

Gabriel: No!

Everyperson: Well. People. Would you credit it?

Gabriel: You get all ready to tell them the news of the century and they're too busy worrying about their taxes....

Everyperson: Too busy to ask if their baby's going to be the Son of God!

Gabriel: Would you believe it....?

They wander to the side of the stage. Conversation fades to 'Rhubarb, rhubarb'.

Enter the Stage Manager.

Stage Manager: Right, now. That's it, I think - everything's ready. ....Manger here *(adjusts it)* - star up there.... Bit of a rapid pregnancy, this, but never mind.... Right! *(calling)* Everybody on, then!

Joseph, Mary, Small Angels *and* Stage-hands *run on, and the* Stage Manager *gives them mimed last-minute instructions.*

Enter the Innkeeper, *his* Wife *and* Villagers.

Gabriel: *(looking round)* Look – it's all starting!

Stage Manager: Now – are we ready?

Gabriel: We'll need a narrator.

Stage Manager: *(not surprised to see* Gabriel) Narrator?

Gabriel: To fill in the background.

Stage Manager: Of course. *(To* Everyperson) Get a narrator, will you, whoever you are.

Everyperson *goes off and comes back leading the* Narrator.

Gabriel: Just like that!

Gabriel *and* Everyperson *stand aside.*

Narrator: And it came to pass in those days, that there went out a decree from Caesar Augustus, that all the world should be taxed.

Everyperson: Sounds familiar.

Narrator: And all went to be taxed, every one into his own city.

Everyperson: 'Went'? If it was their own city, weren't they there already?

Gabriel: It doesn't mean *their* city, it means the city of their ancestors.

Narrator: And Joseph also went up from Galilee, out of the city of Nazareth, into Judea, unto the city of David, because he was of the house and lineage of David....

Everyperson: Lineage – 'And Jacob begat Joseph, husband of Mary, of whom was born Jesus....' See – if you trace the family tree of Jesus back through David, you've got to go through Joseph....

Gabriel: Sssssssh!

Narrator: ....to be taxed with Mary, his espoused wife, being great with child. And so it was....

Joseph *and* Mary *come forward.*

And so it was that, while they were there, the days were accomplished that she should be delivered.

Gabriel: Isn't it beautiful? 'And so it was that the days were accomplished – ' *(rushes forward)* Let's do it properly, with the innkeeper and his wife and everything – it's so *lovely!*

Stage Manager: We're just about to. Don't be impatient.

Gabriel *stands back, ashamed.*

Softly, the accompaniment to 'Away in a Manger'.

The Innkeeper *comes forward, and we see him turning* Joseph *and* Mary *away, then his* Wife *pleading, and the* Innkeeper *reluctantly showing them to the stable.* Oxen *and* Asses - *cut out, or in costume, if available – come on too.*

During the Narrator's *next speech, the* Stage Manager *goes off, comes back with a doll-baby and gives it openly to* Mary.

Narrator: And she brought forth her first-born son, and wrapped him in swaddling clothes, and laid him in a manger, because there was no room for them in the inn.

Pause. Hold.

Gabriel: Marvellous. Quite bowls you over.

Everyperson: I've been thinking about Mary, though. It must have been hard for her.

Gabriel: Hard?

Everyperson: No modern conveniences. How can I....? Look - there's Mr Smithers in the front row. *(Goes to lead* Mr Smithers *forward)* Mr Smithers, would you mind? *(To the others)* He's a Sanitary Inspector from the Health and Safety Executive. Mr Smithers, this is a stable. A baby has just been born here. Is that a satisfactory arrangement?

Mr Smithers: This – dump? For purposes of midwifery? Never! In the first place, it stinks. In the second place, oxen and asses – disgusting! In the third place, there are no – er – sanitary facilities. Running water, flush toilets, etc. No. No. It definitely won't do. *(Sits down)*

Everyperson: And look – there's the local Clinic Nurse. *(Beckons to a woman in uniform,* Mrs Postlethwaite, *from the front row)* Mrs Postlethwaite, could you give us your opinion, please?

Mrs Postlethwaite: It is my duty to ensure that Baby's needs are fully met, that Mother has the proper training in infant care, that all vitamin supplements are provided, feeding schedules maintained and so on and so forth. *(To* Mary) Now, young lady – I presume you have an automatic washing machine for the nappies? No? Then you'll have to use disposables, or it's back to boil-and-scrub like the bad old days! *(Sits down)*

Everyperson: See? It can't have been very romantic.

Gabriel: No.

Mary: *(coming forward)* And there's something else you've forgotten.

Everyperson: What?

Gabriel: Forgotten?

Mary: There was no midwife. No-one to help me have my first baby. No doctor. No drugs. No-one to cut the cord.

Everyperson: No-one?

Mary: Just Joseph. Modern people think they're pretty good just letting the father watch the birth. Joseph had to do everything.

Mary *sits down.* Everyperson *goes and kneels in front of her, and* Gabriel *stands behind them.*

Everyperson: You're wonderful, Mary. Joseph, you're wonderful too.

Narrator: And his name shall be called Wonderful Counsellor, the Mighty God, the Everlasting Father, the Prince of Peace.

Pause. Hold.

Then Everyperson *and* Gabriel *step out of the scene.*

Everyperson: That's not the end yet, is it?

Gabriel: No – there's the shepherds and the kings to come yet.

Everyperson: You look quite dazed.

Gabriel: I am.

Everyperson: Maybe we need a break. Let's have another carol, then the interval.

Gabriel: Good idea.

Everyperson: Go on, then – announce it.

Gabriel: Me? I'm too shy. Can't one of them announce it?

Joseph: Can we have 'Once in Royal David's City'? It's my favourite.

Gabriel: Lovely – that's my favourite too. *(To audience)* 'Once in Royal' – all right? Then we'll have the interval.

Everyperson: See – you've announced it.

Gabriel: Oh! So I have. *(Starts to conduct the carol)*

Audience and cast all sing through to the end.

ACT II

Lights down.

Orchestra or piano play the introduction to 'The First Nowell'. Members of the cast 'planted' in the first row (Mr Smithers *and* Mrs Postlethwaite) *lead the audience in singing it.*

Dark on stage. Then faint lighting.

Dick, *a shepherd, runs on. He sees the audience and runs off again, calling:*

Dick: Hey! They're waiting! It's time to start.

Light grows. We are on the hill outside Bethlehem.

Enter the Shepherds, *who arrange themselves and stare expectantly up at the sky.*

First Shepherd: When are they due, then?

Second Shepherd: Shouldn't be long now.

Third Shepherd: It's the right kind of night for them. All starry.

Dick: There's something wrong, though. Can't think what, but there's something wrong.

Enter Everyperson *at a distance. She stands watching them.*

First Shepherd: They'd better come soon. I'm getting cold.

Dick *sees* Everyperson.

Second Shepherd: Arc they usually? I mean, angels? Are they generally punctual?

Dick *goes over to* Everyperson.

Third Shepherd: I don't know. I've never been in on this kind of thing before.

Dick: Excuse me. I wonder if you could tell us.

Everyperson: Tell you?

Dick: How long they'll be.

Everyperson: They?

Dick: The angels.

Everyperson: How long they'll be?

Dick: It seems a reasonable question to ask. On a night like this.

Everyperson: It is not a reasonable question to ask! *(Marches over to the* Shepherds) You're not supposed to be expecting them! It's a surprise! 'Fear not' and 'Mighty dread' and all that! Go to sleep or something. Look after your sheep. *(Returns to her corner, muttering)* Would you believe it – just sitting there, waiting....

Dick: Go on, then. Like the lady said. Sleep *(first Shepherd does).* Look for lost sheep *(second Shepherd does).* Mend your crook *(third Shepherd does).*

Enter Gabriel *behind* Everyperson *and tugs at her sleeve.*

Gabriel: Pssst!

Everyperson: What? Gabriel! For heavens' sake!

Gabriel: Are they ready?

Everyperson: You're as bad as they are! Ready, indeed. You come when God sends you, not when they're ready!

Gabriel: All right, all right. I just come on – suddenly?

Everyperson: Suddenly.

Gabriel: Oh. *(Exit)*

The Three Shepherds *give up trying not to look expectant and begin to chat, 'Rhubarb, rhubarb'.* Dick *is still trying.*

Dick: Oh! Look! There's a lost sheep! I must go and rescue it!

He goes off one side, and Gabriel *comes on the other. The* Shepherds *take no notice. Lighting grows over* Gabriel.

Gabriel: Er – hum. *(Louder)* Er – hum!

Everyperson: Louder.

Gabriel: ER HUM!

First Shepherd: Look!

Second Shepherd: What can that be?

Third Shepherd: It's so bright!

First Shepherd: I think it's a –

Second Shepherd: Yes, it's an –

Third Shepherd: An angel!

Gabriel flaps the gold-edge wings.

Er – archangel!

Gabriel: *(suddenly playing the part properly)* Fear not, for behold, I bring you good tidings of great joy, which shall be to all people.

While Gabriel is speaking, other Angels *come and stand round, and we hear Handel's 'Messiah' (numbers 16 and 17, Watkins Shaw edition): 'And suddenly, there was with the angel a multitude of the heavenly host, praising God and saying, Glory to God in the highest.'*

For unto you is born this day in the city of David a Saviour, which is Christ the Lord. And this shall be a sign unto you: you shall find the babe, wrapped in swaddling clothes, lying in a manger'.

At the end, the other Angels *go off.*

First Shepherd: Amazing! Marvellous!

Second Shepherd: We'd better go, then, hadn't we?

Third Shepherd: Where did the angel say? City of David?

First Shepherd: That's Bethlehem.

Second Shepherd: Down there – look – at the bottom of the hill.

Third Shepherd: Great! Let's go and find the Saviour!

They go off, exclaiming 'Think of it – a baby!' 'What's swaddling?' etc.

Everyperson: That was terrific, Gabriel. You can do it, when you relax.

Gabriel: Was I good? It felt good.

Dick *rushes back on.*

Dick: I had to go right over to that cliffy bit there, and the wretched thing was stuck in a thicket.... *(looks round)* Where have they gone? *(To* Everyperson *and* Gabriel) Excuse me, you two. There were some shepherds here. Did you see where they went to?

Gabriel: Er – Bethlehem, I think....

Dick: You're an angel!

Everyperson: An archangel.

Dick: You're Gabriel.

Gabriel: Nice of you to recognise me.

Dick: You've been? And told them? And they've gone?

Gabriel: Yes....

Everyperson: Bad luck.

Dick: I've missed it?

Gabriel: It – um – seems like it.

Everyperson: Disappointing for you.

Dick: I can't have! I can't bear it! They've all had it – that great moment – and the only one who's missed it is me!

Gabriel: I could do you a re-run? I don't know if I can get the other angels back....

Dick: I don't want a re-run! I want the real thing! It's not fair – I've missed it – *(cries)*

Gabriel: I would have waited if I'd known, really I would.

Everyperson: Stop carrying on like that. You're not the only one who's missed it.

Dick: I am! Off they go to Bethlehem, without me....

Everyperson: Now listen to me, young man. See all that lot, out there *(indicates the audience)*? They have to live the whole of their lives without seeing angels ever. They say their prayers, go to church sometimes - anyway, they try to lead a good sort of life, on the whole. You'd think they'd get a visit from an angel occasionally, wouldn't you, to give them a bit of encouragement? But no. Not a flicker of an angelic feather.

Gabriel: Must be disheartening for them. No wonder they have a jamboree every Christmas, to set themselves up for the rest of the year.

Everyperson: So stop moaning, shepherd. Anyway, there's something you can do.

Dick: Really? What?

Everyperson: Think of a carol for that lot *(indicates audience)* to sing while this lot *(indicates cast)* get ready for the next bit.

Dick: Choose a carol? I know which one!

Everyperson: Which?

Dick: 'While shepherds watched'. Everybody knows that one.

Gabriel: Our baby angels have a joke about that. They sing 'While shepherds washed their socks by night'.

Everyperson: Gabriel! Don't be so irreverent! Isn't he awful?

Dick: Dreadful. *(To audience)* All right, everyone? 'While shepherds watched'.

Accompaniment, then the audience sing.

Lights dim. Exit Everyperson *and* Gabriel.

Dick *sings lustily, and when he has got the audience going, he exits, still singing.*

During the last verse, Everyperson *comes back, disconsolate, and sits down. As the carol ends:*

Everyperson: 'All glory be to God on high – and to the earth be peace....' What does it mean? Does it mean anything to people? Am I nuts even to ask?

Behind her, the Three Kings *walk on in line, bearing their gifts.*

She turns round and sees them, then turns back again.

Hello, hello, hello – now we've got this lot. *(To the* Kings) Who are you?

Caspar: Isn't it obvious?

Melchior: After all that making-up?

Balthazar: We are the three kings.

Everyperson: The three wee kings, as they say in Scotland. Kings – right. *(To* Caspar) Where are you king *of*?

Caspar: Of?

Everyperson: Kings are always of somewhere. Tibet, Upper Volta, Cambodia.

Melchior: We're not that sort of king. We're magi.

Everyperson: Magi? What are they?

Balthazar: Sort of astrologers.

Everyperson: Oh – gypsies in tents with crystal balls. That's rather different from being kings.

Melchior: Astrologers were very important in those days. They didn't have psychologists or economists then – not even weather forecasters. We had to do all that.

Caspar: Best to call us 'Wise Men'.

Everyperson: You are, are you - wise? What are those things you're carrying?

Melchior: Gifts for the baby.

Everyperson: Babies love presents. What have you got, then?

Melchior: *(standing forward)* I bring him gold.

Everyperson: Not a rattle, or a duck to float in his bath?

Melchior: Gold – symbol of wealth, power, and earthly glory. *(Stands back)*

Everyperson: 'Sell all you have and give to the poor – easier for a camel to go through the eye of a needle than a rich man to enter heaven....'

Caspar: Ssssh! *(Standing forward)* I bring him frankincense.

Everyperson: What *is* frankincense?

Caspar: Symbol of holiness, of sacredness, of being set apart from the world. *(Stands back)*

Everyperson: Set apart? The baby, lying in the hay, among the farm animals?

Balthazar: Sssssh! *(Standing forward)* I bring him myrrh.

Everyperson: What do you do with myrrh?

Balthazar: Myrrh is for anointing the dead before they are placed in the tomb.

Everyperson: This is a birth, and you have brought death.

Balthazar: Birth, and death – they come to each one of us. *(Stands back)*

Everyperson: Gold, frankincense and myrrh. Which way are you going? Where does the star lead you?

Caspar: First we're going to see Herod. He's the king of Israel.

Balthazar: Actually, he's a puppet.

Melchior: The Romans are the real rulers. Herod has to do what he's told.

Everyperson: That sort are the worst – the ones who aren't really powerful but pretend they are. You're going to see him?

Caspar: We're going to ask him where the baby is, the one who is born to be king of the Jews.

Balthazar: One king, you see, should be able to tell us where another king is born. Shouldn't he?

Everyperson: You did call yourselves 'wise' men?

Melchior: You – you don't think we're making a mistake, do you?

Everyperson: I'm not sure. Better call the Narrator.

Enter Narrator.

Matthew chapter 2, please. *(She goes and sits apart)*

Narrator: Here begins the second chapter of St Matthew's gospel, beginning at verse one. *(Clears throat)* Now when Jesus was born –

During this reading, Herod *comes on with* Priest/s *and* Scribe/s. *The* Stage Manager *comes on with a throne, and* Herod *sits on it.*

– in Bethlehem of Judea in the days of Herod the king, behold, there came wise men from the east to Jerusalem –

The Kings *come before him.*

– saying....

Caspar:	Where is he that is born king of the Jews?
Balthazar:	For we have seen his star in the east.
Melchior:	And are come to worship him.
Narrator:	When Herod had heard these things, he was troubled *(he is)* and all Jerusalem with him *(they are).* And when he had gathered all the chief priests and scribes of the people (Herod *summons them*) he demanded of them where Christ should be born (Herod *does*). And they said unto him....
Priest:	In Bethlehem of Judea, for so it is written by the prophet.
Narrator:	Then Herod, when he had privily called the wise men, inquired of them diligently (Herod *does*) what time the star appeared. And he sent them to Bethlehem and said....
Herod:	Go and search diligently for the young child; and when ye have found him, bring me word again, that I may come and worship him also.
Narrator:	And when they had heard the king, they departed.

The Kings *walk away and stand apart.*

Enter the Stage Manager, *who shoos off* Herod *and* Courtiers, *and then carries the throne off.*

And lo, the star, which they saw in the east, went before them, till it came and stood over where the young child was. *(Exit)*

Everyperson: *(to the* Kings) So now you know. The baby will be in Bethlehem.

Caspar: Wasn't he pleasant?

Everyperson: Herod?

Balthazar: Really helpful. The chief priests and scribes summoned specially to help us.

Melchior: There was a sort of – look in his eye, though....

Enter Gabriel, *running.*

Gabriel: I've just seen that lot! Herod and his crowd! They were looking ever so pleased with themselves – *(stops in front of the* Kings) You three. You haven't been, have you? To see Herod?

Caspar: We....

Balthazar: We had to go and ask him where....

Melchior: You didn't tell us not to!

Gabriel *puts head in hands.*

Caspar: He wasn't being helpful?

Gabriel: No.

Balthazar: He won't go and worship him also?

Gabriel: No.

Melchior: He'll do something dreadful instead?

Gabriel: He wants to kill him.

Melchior: Kill him?

Balthazar: He's only a baby!

Caspar: He'll do no harm to anybody!

Everyperson: Isn't there something you can do, Gabriel?

Gabriel: Yes. 'When you have seen the young child, with Mary his mother, and have presented unto him your gifts – do not return unto Herod, but depart into your own country another way'. That's right, isn't it? It's the only thing to do, don't you think?

Caspar: Yes.

Balthazar: We'll do that.

Melchior: Thank you very much, Gabriel.

The Kings *bow in turn and go off.*

Everyperson: Terrible, isn't it?

Gabriel: All that power, against a baby.

Everyperson: Herod hates him.

Gabriel: Powerful people will always hate him.

Everyperson: I read about what happened to him in the end.

Gabriel: They tortured him, and killed him.

Everyperson: That's not usually mentioned in Nativity plays.

Gabriel: Because it's so dreadful.

Everyperson: But we should talk about it! If he hadn't been that kind of person, willing to die for what was most important in the whole world, we wouldn't be celebrating his birth now.

Gabriel: We wouldn't have Nativity plays at all.

Lights dim. Orchestra or piano plays, very softly, 'O little town of Bethlehem', while the entire cast come on. Stage-hands *come and finish the manger and other props. Much busyness: the* Stage Manager *comes on carrying something and rushes around and off the other side, then on again without it – a* Small Angel *rushes off and is dragged back on by a larger* Angel *– etc., ad lib, till the whole Nativity scene is arranged.*

Stage Manager: *(in a stage whisper)* Now, everyone – ten seconds! Becky, straighten that halo! You angel over there, I can see your trainers sticking out underneath! And for the last time, everybody – no waving to Mums or Dads in the audience! Right! Lights! *(Runs to the side)*

Enter Narrator.

Full lights. The classic Nativity scene.

Narrator: And when they were come in, they saw the young child with Mary his mother.

The Shepherds *and the* Kings *come in turn and lay their gifts in front of the manger.*

And they fell down and worshipped him.

Choir, or a few of the cast, sing quietly: 'How silently, how silently' from 'O little town of Bethlehem'.

During the singing, Gabriel *and* Everyperson *come nearer and gaze at the scene.*

As the singing ends, a short pause, then:

Everyperson: Are you pleased with it, then, Gabriel? A bit proud of yourself?

Gabriel: Mostly I got it all wrong. But if I stopped worrying, the right bits happened by themselves.

Everyperson: But – have we actually been back in Bethlehem? Or is this just play-acting, two thousand years later?

Gabriel: Maybe it's both.

Everyperson: I wanted the real thing – the real meaning. But this is a sham! In ten minutes, all that lot'll be quarrelling, and writing 'I want this, I want that' to Santa Claus.

Gabriel: What difference does it make?

Everyperson: Look – if that was God, he'd jump out of the manger and stop us being angry and greedy and fighting wars. A baby! What use is that?

Gabriel: He offered us the kingdom of God. We can choose it, or say no to it, as we like.

Everyperson: Choose?

Gabriel: He won't do it for us. It's not easy – you know how his life ended.

Everyperson: On a cross. But he was special! There

was God in him. There's no way we can be like that.

Gabriel: There's something in us, too. Even in stupid me, even in quarrelsome you. Can't you feel it, Everyperson? When you're quiet enough to hear your heart beating, when you're with friends and you love them? Can't you feel that light, that love inside you?

Everyperson: You mean.... that?

Gabriel: 'The kingdom of God is within you'.

Silence. Then suddenly Gabriel *claps hands.*

Hey – I got it right! Didn't I, Mary?

Mary: *(coming over)* You got it right, Gabriel.

Mary *takes hands with* Gabriel *and* Everyperson.

Introduction to 'In the bleak midwinter'.

(singing) What can I give him,
Poor as I am?
If I were a shepherd,
I would bring a lamb.
If I were a wise man,
I would do my part –
Yet, what I can, I give him –
Give my heart.

The actors lead the audience in singing the whole carol.

QUESTIONS FOR DISCUSSION

1 Does it matter who Jesus's f/Father was (page 16)? Try and answer this for yourself, without trying to think what is the 'right' or 'wrong' answer.

Can you imagine Jesus joining in the argument?

If you feel very strongly one way or the other, ask yourself whether you've come to this conclusion:

(a) because of your wide knowledge of the Bible and of biblical criticism;

(b) because you need to believe it at this stage of your development of mind or spirit;

(c) because your family or teachers have given the belief (or lack of it) to you.

2 Why, when Jesus was born in a stable (imagine it – a stable!) are Western Christian countries well-fed and rich while other countries in the world are in a disastrous situation of starvation and disease?

Why are Christian churches themselves so wealthy? What did Jesus, when he grew up, say about wealth and poverty, and what does it really mean, now, for us? (see page 34)

Do you feel guilty even thinking about these questions? If you do, join the club! But try and find your personal answer – some small or large action that you can take, some attitude you can change. Best of all, try and imagine what it might be like to be as desperate for food and shelter as Joseph and Mary were when they arrived in Bethlehem that night.

3 Is it true (page 38) that 'powerful people will always hate him'? What about governments that declare their Christianity? If Jesus came to this country, today, would he be welcomed? What do you think he might say

(a) to you?

(b) to the leaders of your school or church?

(c) to those who run industry, the professions, the country?

4 In your experience, is the Christmas story something you grow out of, like Father Christmas?

What place does Jesus's birth take in your Christmas, when there's so much else to think about – shopping, tinsel, tree and turkey to buy, that present for Uncle George (you bought him socks and a tie *last* year), what you're going to ask everyone else to give you – the school/church play...?

...We celebrate it every year. But what does it mean, to you?